Poetic Collections Of AnanthaShri

English poems covering some of the Social and Emotional Aspects

Vemuri Anantha Ramakrishna...

BookLeaf Publishing

India | USA | UK

Made with ❤ on the BookLeaf Publishing Platform
www.bookleafpub.in
www.bookleafpub.com

Dedication

To my loving family, whose unwavering love and support have always been my guiding light. To my parents, who taught me the power of resilience and the importance of dreaming big. To my father-in-law and friends and mentors, whose belief in me never faltered, and whose patience kept me grounded through the highs and lows of this journey.

And to the countless storytellers—past and present—who have inspired me to pick up the pen and share my own voice.

Preface

Writing this book has been a journey—one filled with moments of inspiration, doubt, clarity, and discovery. It began as a simple idea, sparked by a question, an observation, or perhaps just a fleeting thought. But as these early fragments began to take shape, the need to explore and share what I had uncovered became undeniable.

In these pages, you will find a blend of research, personal experience, and reflection. For some, the concepts may be familiar, but I hope they spark new insights. For others, this may be an entirely new path to walk down. Either way, my hope is that it resonates with you in some way.

This book is not meant to be the definitive answer to any of the questions it raises. Rather, it is an invitation to think, to question, and to explore. It is a reflection of my own journey, and as with any journey, it is far from complete.

I want to acknowledge that writing this book was never a solitary endeavor. It was shaped by the voices of mentors, friends, colleagues, and countless strangers whose thoughts and ideas I encountered along the way. While I take full responsibility for the words on these pages, I am indebted to the many people who helped me find my way here.

Finally, to you, the reader: I thank you for taking the time to read these words. I hope they spark something within you—whether it's a thought, a feeling, or a new perspective. This book is yours now as much as it is mine.

Acknowledgements

I am deeply grateful to my wife who has been the source
of inspiration in choosing the topics that were addressed
and my experiences with my children which helped me
further to refine the topics and other social and
emotional issues that contributed to it. I thank my
friends and family who have been helpful and
contributed with their constructive feedback

1. Breath of Life

When a breath fills a mother's womb
signalling a new life on earth
Gods creation takes centrefold spanning earth's length
and breadth

Parents prepare themselves for a long haul
As their earnest prayers are answered by god's call

Its a culmination of nine months of parent's ordeal
As its a real deal and no scent is more fragrant than the
scent of a baby's feel

As the baby makes an effort to come out and the room is
filled with the mother's shout
The father waits with a bated breath for the baby to
come out

Our worlds are filled with absolute silence
As the baby makes way to mark its presence

Parents are reminded of life's essence as they start their
life with new effervescence
Parents travel with ecstasy through the ethereal heavens

Before they are brought back to earth through doctor's
summons
Parents are made to fill forms of their consent

Before the mother starts feeding the baby to her heart's
content
Holding the baby the mothers joy knows no bounds,

As father prepares a list by making repeated rounds
Before they leave the hallowed hospital grounds,

Life would have come a full circle just by hearing the
baby's sounds
No words can describe what parents went through as the
feeling of their greatest accomplishment stays true

Happiness descends on their faces as cool as moonlight
And the light of their joy blocks even the rays of
sunlight

While they make their way out of the hospital to make
space (for others)
Eager to get away keeping their prize possession in place

Mysterious is breath's journey and more mysterious are
gods ways
As his smile shines through the baby's face

Nothing can compare to a mother's loving gaze
Unfathomable as the secret of life as always

2. Color of Humanity

Eyes are meant to enjoy the beauty of nature
Not to see the color of skin and give a racist's signature
Color of skin is transient and commutable
But the color of soul is eternal and immutable
Judging people through color only diminishes human
stature

We have five senses for different reasons
Not just to enjoy seasons across regions
But to differentiate between right and wrong
To nurture life and let the good nature to prolong
Afterall, being sensible is how we owe mankind our
allegiance

What's the use of sulking over skin's color?
If you cannot revel in life's true flavor
Dont waste the gift of senses to falsely influence your
mind
Make good use of your intellect to leave discrimination
behind

Its your bounden duty to do humanity a favor

Gloating over having fair skin will only last till your eyes
are closed
As it can only conceal the darkness of your heart that
stands exposed
Its not the color of skin that defines a person but the
color of their character
One that can leave an indelible mark as humanity's
greatest benefactor
The world would end up being a better place if everyone
gets on board

3. Relation

What is a relation?
Nothing but a sweet and beautiful connection.

Relaying Heart's emotion,
With someone showing affection.

An Elation felt through mutual actions,
Or Despair felt through conflicting reactions.

Relations linked through money aren't sound,
But those linked through emotions will make you bound.

Relations driven by intellect will always become
conditional,
Relations driven by right emotion will always become
cordial.

Identity is always related to someone or something,
Efforts are made to keep it that way before it turns to
nothing.

Importance is given to blood relations, arising out of
trust,
But along the line, mind and heart attaches more to
emotional thrust.

Relation doesn't need a name or address to connect,
Its the happiness in your heart that it reflects.

Humanity sustains only through relations that makes us
sentient,
Technology is only meant to augment positive relations
not fragment.

4. Power of Love

My day started with eyes refusing to open and the
nature's warm but subtle winds causing my heart to
flutter.
One lazy glance at your ethereal beauty by my side
quieted my inner voice and caused my words to stutter

The splendor emanating from your cherubic smile has
every cell in my body basking in its glory,
Such is the impact of your presence that it is making
every moment of my life a lasting memory

The gaiety in my heart goes up by leaps and bounds,
My dear, Listening to your mellifluous voice.
Culminating in an ecstasy that astounds,
Leaving a lasting feeling that rolls me up in boundless
joys.

Whenever I sense an unwanted moment of your silence,
my heart ululates,albeit brief,
Only to heave a sigh of relief looking at your angelic

face.
My heart screams out loud trying to break these silent
shackles of grief,
My breath undulates and returns to normalcy by clearing
the mind's cluttered space.

As you walk through the aisle wiggling your slender
hips,
Thou shalt not kill is a commandment your piercing gaze
donot seem to follow,
It feels as though the lake of life's elixir is opened for
little dips,
I find myself drowning, struggling to breathe and urging
you to go slow.

Fully drenched in your love, my heart longs to bask in
the warmth of your embrace,
Turning everything trivial which seemed so dear a
moment ago.
With all unpleasant memories my heart held appear to
be effaced,
Your endearing smile redefines my life's purpose and
deals a crushing blow to my unflinching ego.

5. True Friend

Seek happiness by filling your life with a dose of
friendship
Whether be a parent or an heir apparent always be
aboard the ship of friendship

Having a true friend by your side is something you will
never regret
Happy times spent with them are some that would be
hard to forget

When you are at crossroads in your life's journey
One road might lead you to unexplainable Agony

One road might lead you to perfect Harmony
Stay put with your friend and the road always leads to
true joy

Beauty is only in the eyes of the beholder
But Friendship is in the heart of the caring shoulder

Beauty might make an impression that is skin deep
But Friendship makes an impression that is for one's to
keep

All in all,To describe friendship , words may well come
up short
Albeit,friendship is such that it can make words to touch
one's heart

Regardless of what you give, a true friend always takes
you by his stride
Regardless of what you do, an enemy would always take
you for a ride

There may be innumerable enemies like the stars in the
sky who always have something to hide
But its not easy to cajole someone who has a true friend
by his side

6. Nature's Quintet

Oh man!
Give me a break,
Doesn't it ring a bell,
Life is getting complicated
Every Day.

Beware,
Clock is ticking,
Know this before too late,
Time and tide waits for no one,
Look back,

We are,
Toying big time,
With nature knowingly
Paying dearly quite too often,
Unmoved,

Careless,
Self indulgent,

Crossing all known limits,
Boasting In the name of progress,
Two words,

No more,
See around us,
Our World is not the same,
Conditions getting more gloomier
To live.

How much,
More can we take,
Before it dawns on us,
Respect our surroundings for once,
Take charge.

Clean up,
Our acts affect
Future generations,
Give them a better world to live,
Last call,

Wake up,
Time to grow up,
Our only way to survive?
Be responsible and careful,
Own up.

7. Modern day India

Not long ago, there was a mad rush to go and settle in
America at any cost
Leaving behind everything they held dear for long
assuming all is lost
Considered America as their most favorable final
destination
Left India and chalked out their destiny to be part of that
nation
Many realised that times change and their short lived
dreams won't last

As economy opened up and technology boom made an
impact on people's lives
Country took a giant leap forward to become the place
everyone loves
People started splurging money on luxuries
To be a part of modern day success stories
Reminding us of the golden age and bring back those lost
smiles

Gone are the days when people used in line up in long
queues to get a Visa
Even paying someone to stand in the line for them thats
how we saw
Now with internet and everything well connected
Experience became digital and duly selected
Their unforeseen fortunes going back and forth like a
seesaw

The lure of the dollar and its buying power reached its
peak
Pushing parents and students into a debt trap they
daren't speak
Money can buy many things but not people's emotions
Recession played its part to quell such unrealistic notions
Unveiling a world of prospects which were once
considered bleak

India started to become the land of startups
Pushing new entrepreneurs to pull out all stops
The power of AI has taken control of you and I
Showing there is more to IT than meets the eye
To fulfill one's dreams and make it only a life of ups

8. Patience

Patience is a virtue that is essentially lacking in people
these days

Its a dog eat dog world out there and a race against time
in many ways

To be able to absorb pressure and stress may not be
everybody's cup of tea

And to come out unscathed might be difficult to achieve
and beyond their capacity

Its time we slow down and strive to make the world a
better place

People these days are becoming ruder and cruder by the
way

Irritating enough to be louder and more grumpier by the
day

Said a pedestrian,while walking on the road

Sad at the current state and ready to unload

Losing patience with his inability to deal with reality and
drifting away

Where does this leave an idle man or an idle mind? You
might ask

Probably at a devil's workshop trying to peel off his lazy
mask

To be considered inclusive in the society might be a hard
nut to crack

Affected by the sea of change and struggling to get back
on track

Patience is their only tool against this herculean task

Running around daily chores and trying to make a name
aptly defines today's man

Not hesitating in the least to ponder if his actions are
aligned with nature's plan

Turn back, O man before its too late says nature

Be patient, it serves as a bad omen for your near future

Leaving future generations in jeopardy and put an end to
insensible actions if you can

9. Wish

Wishful thinking is a healthy habit which helps in
instilling hope and optimism in us
A positive thought emerging from the innermost part of
your soul before the door for its fruition closes
Wish is kept alive through sheer determination before
the fire to fulfill it extinguishes
Wish fills our heart with happiness and opens the door
to new horizons

Wish all you want add fervour and you're ready to
pursue
If you wish to manifest it sooner add your will power to
realise it for sure
A heartfelt wish never goes abegging as it carries a ray
of hope to dispel the dark
Good intentions hit their mark as divine blessings add to
the spark

Wish manifests as reality when there is a will to show its
way

A simple wish has so much say that it takes a child's
happy face to get blown away
Make hay while sun shines and fulfill the wish when
your heart pines
Unfulfilled wish creates negative vibes and a gloomy
outlook of our life's confines

World is a better place to live when the collective wishes
of people turn to realities
So much so that they do not pay heed to each other's
frailties
We cant stop making a wish seeing a shooting star
because we cant stop ourselves
Whether a wish comes true or remains a dream entirely
depends on one's belief in oneself

10. Beauty is only skin deep

Beauty is only skin deep when looked at in retrospect
But it makes an impression heart deep when you first
inspect
To describe beauty, words may well come up short
But it can definitely make your words to touch one's
heart

Beauty is in the eyes of the beholder only when you
have an eye for appreciating beauty in the first place
For someone to grab your attention beauty comes in
your line of sight when you look at someone's face
Beauty always takes centerstage as it fills up your entire
mind space
Slowly pulling up your innermost feelings to the front at
its own pace

Some say look at one's inner beauty felt through ever
lasting emotions
Stay put with the person in question as your heart sinks
into beauty's unfathomable oceans

As their character grows on you the impression it made
on your heart abets your mind's preconceived notions
Then beauty no longer becomes physical but more
spiritual when heart resolves all unanswered questions

Eyes can discern thousands of colors but cannot discern
the color of heart
Heart can discern thousands of feelings but cannot
discern when to stop
Mind processes what heart discards but cannot discern
when emotions will pop
Only when mind and heart are in the right place the real
beauty of emotions plays its part

11. Rain rain go away come again another day

Not long ago, humanity faced and still facing its greatest
crisis in the pandemic
One that sent a chill down everyone's spine that one
couldn't still depict
To get normal seasonal rainfall has become a distant
thing in the past
Rain accompanied with the pain of losing someone is
becoming really hard to digest

Without water there is no life on earth which is the
universal truth
Its unthinkable if the same water changes from life
saving to threatening without any ruth
All these days mankind assumed nature would align
itself around us and follow
Contrary to the expectations, our understanding proved
to be too hollow

Repeatedly reminding us of calamities has really become

nature's second nature
Trying to make us understand without endangering our
promising future
Encroaching water bodies was thought of as a sign of
progress by some to embark
Little did we realise that without natural water bodies,
our existence would itself become a question mark

Our childhood is filled with so many beautiful memories
with the first advent of rain
When a memory would become a nightmare might
become too hard for our future generations to explain
To err is human but to respect nature
is what makes us human
As long as this thought is etched in our heart, there is
some hope for everyone

12. Guru

Teacher is someone who doesnt just teach but connects
to your heart to reach
Teacher is someone who doesn't just reproach but
corrects your approach
Teacher is someone who doesn't just guide but teaches
you how to abide
Teacher is someone who doesn't just stand by your side
but bridges the knowledge to ignorance divide

Mother is your first teacher who teaches you the ways of
the world
Father teaches you discipline and hones your skills to
keep them as sharp as a sword
A teacher imparts knowledge to you to survive and
educate on redundant things you need to forego
Regardless of who teaches us they all strive towards
taking us where we would like to go

Let the education be elementary or primary, high school
or higher studies

Teacher walks with you till your career ship steadies
No amount of wealth can compensate the wealth of
knowledge you acquire
For that a good teacher who knows you in and out is all
you require

Respecting the teachers is the first lesson that we should
learn
Without them we all would end up in the world of
darkness and burn
Teacher is the light that dispels darkens and gives our
life a delightful turn
I bow to the divine that is embodied in teachers
deserving all the respect they earned

13. Louis Braille

In dark rooms, where sight has no say,
A precocious boy imagined, words can still come into
play.
Of tales told, gain insights to become one of a kind,
A world of difference, it can make to those blind .

Devoid of sight as a child, his spirit unbroken,
Unhampered by disability, his wisdom awakened.
He chose a path, unforeseen before,
To pave the way , where minds can explore .

Driven by an undying spirit and a helping hand,
He chose to become the saviour of blind.
Inspired by military code, came the raised dots that stood
the test of time
Where millions benefited as a gift from divine.

As mankind took a giant leap into technology,
A new world emerged for the blind to become part of
main stream topology.

Where blind can not only read but make a difference,
And looked upon with reverence.

Kudos to the man, whose thought shone so bright,
That shed light on the blind's plight
Louis Braille, your name will shine for eternity ,
As an inspiration and a beacon of humanity.

14. Inner Strength

When the chips are down,
Showing no signs of slowing down,
Despair spreading its wings,
Casting a spell of gloom that stings.

Within the deep confines of the heart,
A glimmer of hope starts to flicker, promising a fresh
start.
All of a sudden, something starts feeling right.
To wade through difficult times with a fight.

For Mind when bogged down by failure,
Everything feels dubious and unsure.
True test of one's character begins,
With a show of inner strength that always wins.

Armed with a new resolve,
Any problem in life, ready to solve.
No matter how tricky the road ahead seems,
Nothing comes in way to realizing your dreams.

Though darkness seems to have a hold every night,
Beyond its every tunnel, there is ray of light to keep you
afloat.
Pitted against destiny, all might seem to be against your
wishes,
But the lamp of your inner strength, though might
appear out, never diminishes.

15. Student's GRE Odyssey

Abasing oneself to get vocabulary power was an act of
abashment that went unabated during our college days.
Those who abstained from this saved themselves from
this affliction and parted ways.
Substituting Abhorrence for hating such actions while
speaking was so abominable,
It required performing verbal ablutions to cleanse
ourselves of local dialects to sound amiable.

Some remained aloof to the allure of land of opportunity,
Some were left Agape, aghast and agog and looked at
with impunity.
Those who were too eager to realise their dreams went
with such an alarming alacrity,
That their efforts were commendable and treated with
dignity.

Accosting others with their new found power often led
to bewilderment and a sense of chagrin for others.
Who still remembers the travails and tribulations to get a

good score in GRE and Toefl with honours.
Rummaging through Rosen Blum, Wilfred Funk and
Barrons for getting the vocabulary power,
Was an exercise so intense and exhausting that it sent
down a shiver.

Some students were under the able aegis of seniors,
But were either cajoled to write or crumbled under peer
pressure of their juniors.
For some learning words was like a legerdemain taught
by vocabulary thaumaturgists,
For some it was a neverending story that left them
ambivalent and failed to get the gist.

All understood chemistry to some extent but never
found the right time to use alchemy.
All these GRE words attenuated some and made them
visit an apothecary.
Making them averse to abetting their children and be
more realistic,
And not go through odysseys that might sound totally
atavistic.

Thought of basking under the azure skies of rustic village
environment
But got compelled to spit out these forgotten memoirs to
establish a new argot.

Not sure about reaching the acme of accomplishments,
But definitely enables you to give speeches with right
embellishments.

Thanks GRE for messing with us.

16. Foreign Life

Are you planning to study abroad for a bright future by
getting a Visa?
Dont be surprised if got beset by troubles you never
foresaw
Life can go back and forth without a hold like a seesaw
Tantalising and puzzling like a jigsaw

Life can take a lot of twists and might appear to come to
a standstill
Might throw a spanner in your works that were filled
with dreams and desires that may never fulfill
Motherland might become a favorable option to recover
if you swallow a bitter pill
You might thank your lucky stars later if you are looking
for a happiness refill

Past would be dictated by your goals and dreams
Present and the future governed by family dreams
Develop a social sense if routine life is being driven by
frustrating screams

Keep your chin up even when caught unaware of the
lurking dangers if it seems

Try to turn over a new leaf if you want to get something
out of this life
Realise that the world will always be a double edged
knife
Creating a new identity is never too late if accompanied
by passion
At the end it might come down to just one chance to
cash in

17. Wisdom

A wiseman once said wisdom dawns from one's own
experiences
Especially while facing life's problems through refusal to
mend fences
For some it happens early when reality breaches their
inner defences
For some it happens too late when solitude commences

It is for a reason they say wisdom teeth is the last set of
adult teeth that grows
Not everyone has wisdom teeth just like not everyone is
wise and ready for life's highs and lows
Sink your wisdom teeth into handling the challenges life
throws at you then the river of knowledge flows
And once you are aboard the ship of knowledge then the
confidence in you just glows

People might grow financially, physically or socially but
those who grow mentally will have the final say
Wisdom is power and to make wise use of its power

your character will be tested to the core for assay
Life presents a lot of opportunities that come your way
that have a lot of say
Making use of these will fortify your mental strength
and keeps unsavory moments away

Wisdom is what differentiates humans from other
species
Through the wise sense of humanity the burden on
nature to maintain ecological balance eases
By taking wise decisions discerning right from wrong
the animalistic tendencies in us ceases
Which in recent times has left a lot to be desired in terms
of humanitarian responses

18. Patriotism

Patriotism is not just a word that means love for your
country
Its not a duty that people can casually do perfunctory
Its a feeling that dictates the progress of a nation and
one that is so rudimentary
A beacon that stands the test of time and makes actions
towards your country involuntary

Patriotism is not a speech that people tend to give while
talking on the stage
Its not something nation beseeches you to feel till you
get to old age
Its not a sermon that you preach to others but a
mandatory social language
Its an innate feeling of belonging that drives your heart
and mind to freely engage

Patriotism is an action so pure and sacred that it sans
egoism
Which during the moment of crisis demands certain

heroism
A deed so noble among people that it doesnt lead people
to gravitate towards jingoism
A mandatory sense of action that allows people to rise
above the cultural and diversity macrocosm

Patriotism is not a concept taught to children through
words but lessons imbibed through actions
Patriotism is not a political agenda that gets manifested
during elections
Its a sense of collectiveness that serves as a construct for
future generations
A pledge that one needs to honor for life and one that
defines nations

19. Good Old School Days

How nostalgic are those moments when we look back at
our school days?
So pristine in its ambience and so blissful for us to face.

Ringing of a school bell does ring a bell if one
reminisces,
When we as children used to enter the school premises.
Every day entering our classroom was filled with zest
and full of promise,
That had our share of eventful days which we never gave
a miss.

Pretending to listen to our teachers led to a lot of funny
encounters some we remember till date,
Withstanding the standing on the bench for talking in
the class or kneeling down till the class is over for
coming late.
Teachers always had something up their sleeves
everyday as soon as they got inside the school gate,
Ad hoc tests given to expose the gaps in our preparation

and put us to shame that we always used to hate.

Not doing homeworks in time and giving dumb excuses
created so much trouble,
That it took all our efforts and wit so that teachers dont
pop the bubble.
Still that was a habit we carried all the way from
primary school to middle school and middle school to
high school,
Doing anything on time is a valuable lesson that some of
us could inculcate and put it to good use as a life
defining career tool.

Examinations were the hardest part especially when we
used to get our report card,
Lot of us too scared to look and getting the parents to
sign it which was so hard.
As time flew by everyone had to go through the dreaded
public examination,
Which held our fate that prepared all of us to face the
real world and be part of college and life education.

So precious were those school days filled with happiness
and sweet memories that we currently lack,
Not a day goes by without thinking what if there is a
time machine for all of us to go back.
We advanced so much in terms of technology that we

started depending on artificial intelligence,
But no technology can bring back the innocence of
childhood and its effervescence.

How nostalgic are those moments when we look back at
our school days,
So pristine in its ambience and so blissful for us to face.

20. Festival of Crackers

Not often you can get to say its a cracker of a festival
Now is the right time to say it out loud it is the festival
of crackers
The moment of truth has arrived to dispel the darkness
and light the bonfire for the festival of lights
Bursting fire crackers by the dozen might just give you
the bragging rights

People in every city and village will be bustling with
activity eager to buy crackers with elan
Behold the light that spelt the doom of evil and served as
a festive beacon
Get on the bandwagon of optimism and positivity and
fight with the doomsayers head-on
The world is filled with a legion of wiseacres and is in
dire need of humanity to carry-on

Nations are on a collision course to destroy everything in
the name of sovereignty
It is about time people understand the gravity of the

situation and step in to restore parity
Let diwali light the lamp of realisation and bring in the
much needed clarity
May common sense prevail and rain festive showers
with a touch of reality

Happy Diwaali to all

21. Dreams

The best way to judge how your day went is how good
you slept at night
When lucid dreams transport your soul to other worlds
which are a true delight
People say I had a very good sleep but fail to recollect
what felt right
When you get a good dream your body goes to rest and
your mind will take flight

Dreams are a way to relive your thoughts that need a
closure
Thoughts that were meant to bore fruit but failed to get
exposure
Things may not turn out the way you want during the
day
But dream all you want at night as moon shines and you
might still make hay

Living a dream life is what everyone wants so they say
But making the dream come true is even harder to attain

per se
Realising your dreams requires utmost focus and
keeping everything else at bay
Once your dream becomes reality your success and
happiness is here to stay

How nice if dream making can become affordable and
customizable
All dreams may not come true but some can make it
believable
If only it can allow us to stay back in those dreams a bit
longer
For what is a dream it is just as real as our waking state
only shorter